Anonymous

An Ancient Syriac Document

Part 1

Anonymous

An Ancient Syriac Document
Part 1

ISBN/EAN: 9783337258672

Printed in Europe, USA, Canada, Australia, Japan

Cover: Foto ©Suzi / pixelio.de

More available books at **www.hansebooks.com**

AN

ANCIENT SYRIAC DOCUMENT,

PURPORTING TO BE THE RECORD, IN ITS CHIEF FEATURES, OF

THE SECOND SYNOD OF EPHESUS,

AND DISCLOSING HISTORICAL MATTER

'INTERESTING TO THE CHURCH AT LARGE;'

Of which Document an attempt at an entire Reproduction in Fac-simile Characters
and at a Translation is now first made

BY THE

REV. S. G. F. PERRY, M.A.

ܐܣܛܠ ܚܬ ܐܠܘܢܝ ܐܦ ܐܚܟܐ ܡܠܒܩܡ
ܚܡܠ: ܐܚܡ ܐܝܠ ܚܡܠܗܘܩ.

(Dr. Samuel Lee's Syriac N. T.)

PART I.

OXFORD

BY T. COMBE, M.A., E. B. GARDNER, E. P. HALL, AND H. LATHAM, M.A.

𝕻rinters to the 𝖀niversity

1867

TO

THE HOLY SYNOD OF BISHOPS

OF CHRIST'S HOLY CATHOLIC CHURCH,

MOST REVEREND AND RIGHT REVEREND FATHERS IN GOD

IN COMMUNION WITH THE SEE OF CANTERBURY;

Convoked at the instance of the Metropolitan and Bishops of Canada and of others, and holden at Lambeth Palace on 24, 25, 26, 27th days of September, in the year 1867, under the Presidency of his Grace the Lord Archbishop of Canterbury, in the spirit which animated 'that gentle Father of his People,' who says of 'the Bishops assembled in Council'—'The Divine favour will bring to pass, that we with the rest, our Colleagues, may stably and firmly administer our office, and uphold the peace of the Catholic Church in the unity of concord:' this attempt at an entire reproduction in fac-simile Estrangĕlā characters and at a translation, of

AN ANCIENT SYRIAC DOCUMENT

(for centuries lost, and now generally unknown, to the Church)

purporting to be an historical relation, in its chief features, of a certain Synod at Ephesus summoned by Imperial Authority to be held in August, 449 A. D. as, and distinctly and authoritatively designated by itself when held to be,

AN ŒCUMENICAL SYNOD OF THE CATHOLIC CHURCH,

but, by reason of the outrage committed by its President and the violent perversion of its ends, for ever pronounced by Saint Leo the Great to be the

'LATROCINIUM' OF EPHESUS,

IS,

WITH PROFOUND VENERATION, AS WELL AS BY EXPRESS PERMISSION,

DEDICATED

BY A PRIEST OF THE CATHOLIC CHURCH IN COMMUNION WITH THE SEE OF CANTERBURY.

PREFATORY REMARKS.

THE original ancient Document, which the following pages indicate an attempt to reproduce in fac-simile type and to translate, forms one of those rich and magnificent Syriac treasures which the present Archdeacon of Bedford, Dr. Tattam, brought from the Syrian Monastery of St. Mary Deipara, in the Desert of Nitria or Scete (ܪܚܝܘܩܝ ܕܝܠܗ ܕܝܪܐ ܕܐܡܐ ܝܠܕܬ), on the Western side of the Nile, between twenty and thirty years ago. The most important and most ancient of all those treasures have already been made known to the world by distinguished Oriental scholars, viz.:—

(1) Clementis Romani Recognitiones, by Dr. P. de Lagarde of Berlin.

(2) Titi Bostreni contra Manichæos libri quatuor, by Dr. P. de Lagarde.

(3) Eusebius Bishop of Cæsarea on the Theophania or Divine Manifestation of our Lord and Saviour Jesus Christ, with a translation and notes, by Dr. Samuel Lee, late Professor of Hebrew at Cambridge.

(4) Ancient Syriac Documents relative to the earliest establishment of Christianity in Edessa and the neighbouring countries, from the year after our Lord's Ascension to the beginning of the fourth century, with a translation, by Dr. Cureton, and with a Preface by Dr. William Wright of the British Museum.

(5) Spicilegium Syriacum: containing remains of Bardesan, Meliton, Ambrose, and Mara Bar Serapion, with a translation and notes, by Dr. Cureton.

(6) History of the Martyrs of Palestine, by Eusebius, Bishop of Cæsarea, with a translation into English, and Notes, by Dr. Cureton.

(7) An Ancient Syrian Martyrology, edited and translated by Dr. William Wright of the British Museum, in the Journal of Sacred Literature. 'The MS. of which it forms a part was transcribed in the year of the Greeks 723, i. e. 412 A.D.'

(8) Analecta Syriaca, with Appendix, by Dr. P. de Lagarde.

(9) The Fragments of John of Asia, soon to be published by Dr. J. P. N. Land.

(10) The Festal Letters of St. Athanasius, by Dr. Cureton.

In this last work Dr. Cureton gives a full and very interesting history of the way in which these ancient Syriac monuments were discovered in the Syrian

b

Convent, in the valley of the Nitrian Lakes, and brought by Dr. Tattam in 1842 to England, and afterwards deposited in the British Museum as the property of the nation in 1847, where they now form one of the most remarkable and important collections of the writings of antiquity which have ever been transported from East to West. Dr. Cureton mentions the share M. Pacho had in the purchasing these Manuscripts of the Cloistered Brethren of the Nitrian Valley. It turns out that M. Pacho himself, after having sold, according to agreement, the whole to the trustees of the British Museum, must have withheld part of them in some way or another, of which part the Imperial Public Library of St. Petersburg appears to be in present possession, certainly as far as the Syriac copy of the Ecclesiastical History of Eusebius, which Dr. Wright showed me, is concerned.

Next after these very recherché specimens of Syriac literature above mentioned, ranks in importance and character, as I think, our Manuscript, which describes itself as

ܘܩܡܪܟ ܐܟܐܐܬܝ ܦܐܝܕܝ ܘܩܡܠܘܩ
❖ ܪܐܩܒܪܟ ܘܩܩܡܩܐ ܪܟܐܙܘ ܐܘܩܩܝ

It is most probably a Syriac version, made about a century after the events it records, of a Greek original long since lost to the Church. It is numbered 14,530 among the Additional MSS. in the British Museum. It is very legibly and boldly indited on vellum in the Estrangela character, and presents, as now bound up, only two blank leaves, indicating as few lacunae in the document. The generally excellent condition of the parchment leaves is no doubt due to the continuously dry and warm climate of the Desert, which has preserved it for our benefit during a period considerably exceeding one thousand years, according to the date so fortunately undefaced in this MS., as in many of its fellows, and placed at the end on the last page but one.

The last page, however, presents difficulties of no ordinary kind; but its photographic representative, given in corresponding type at the end of our printed text, magnifying as it does the letters and the parts of letters that are discernible, as well as the marks of disfigurement, may induce some Syriac scholar to venture on an endeavour to decipher the sadly marred features of its dimly sombre visage, and so to offer some solution of those difficulties that have hitherto baffled some few not unskilful handlers of ancient Oriental MSS.

The whole MS. consists of 216 pages, each page averaging about 28 lines. Sometimes towards the middle the lines number 33 and 34. The portion of the Syriac text printed in this Part I is the beginning of the attempt at a reproduction of the document in its entirety, so that, page in our text nearly

corresponding to page in the original, and line exactly to line, word for word, red type for red, and black type for black, we shall be enabled in the course of time, if encouraged, to accomplish the task of reproducing the whole document in fac-simile Estrangēlā characters as contemplated.

The translation strikes off with the Latin rendering of one of the documents already given in Mansi's L'Abbé. The English translation here given points to those very important matters connected with the characteristics of this MS.; for it relates to what occurred after August 8, and to the case of Ibas and to the unfolding of the unlawful acts of Dioscorus and partisans at the Synod, by which its President perverted it into a Conciliabulum and that Conciliabulum into the Latrocinium of Ephesus. The Emperor had summoned the Synod for August 1. Its first session, three extant fragments concerning which are given in Latin and Greek in L'Abbé's 'Conciliorum Collectio,' took place on August 8. It is the Session on Saturday, August 20, of which mention is made, and that on Monday, August 22, proceedings of which are recorded, in these Acts alone.

As the preceding remarks relative to the Syriac MSS. cannot be otherwise than apposite and pertinent to the matter in hand, so the subjoined reflections will not, I think, be considered inapposite or inopportune, which deal with the subject of Synods generally, although *at present* it appears to be not unwise to say little of that particular one, of which *much* is to be said and can be better said when all connected with it is complete.

Now it is evident to all men (ܐܠܗܐ ܪܝܫ ܘ to use the first words of our document) reading the signs of the times, that the grand idea of the distinctive oneness of the 'one Body' of Christ—so fully taught by the Holy Ghost, as well in the glorious Creeds of the Church Catholic as through the direct and immediate inspiration of Holy Writ—is receiving and growing into a vivid realization in this latter half of the nineteenth century, which may witness, before its close, through that 'one Body' being continually quickened and informed by the 'one Spirit,' a no inappreciable approximation to the Church's oneness of character in primitive times. And there is also much reason to aver that the synodical system of the Church, by and in the highest form of which her articulate voice was in the ages of faith so faithfully uttered and obediently heard, and of which, I will add, our MS., coming up as it does through the long vista of those past ages from the unchanging East, is so singularly expressive, promises, by God's mercy to us, to receive such positive and helpful encouragements as will afford to many, yearning for its joyful fulness, a warranty of hope and belief that that visible Oneness or Unity must also be attended with an immediate and manifest accession.

Now the Synodical Institutions of the Church Catholic are of Divine origin. The germ from which they are all evolved and the source to which they can be referred and traced back, as well in their first emergent and scarcely discernible development as in the grandest and most glorious, when the largest General Council could exultingly appropriate Christ's promise to itself, may be found in the Divine words containing that promise of our Lord's gracious Presence : οὐ γάρ εἰσι δύο ἢ τρεῖς συνηγμένοι εἰς τὸ ἐμὸν ὄνομα, ἐκεῖ εἰμι ἐν μέσῳ αὐτῶν. The secondary meaning of those words, reality of belief in which has been abundantly and unprecedentedly evidenced of late years—may it still increase !—in the awakened consciousness of Churchmen to privileges and duties in connection with assemblies for Worship, needs certainly no elaborate elucidation ; whilst the primary, significative of order, discipline, and work, has surely been insufficiently regarded in the realization of blessings inherent of necessity in a guaranteed promise to what is done, εἰς τὸ ὄνομα, by many or by few in authorized union and action.

This year of grace, however, and this month of September, bear witness to a special and unprecedented instance of actual realization of the promise, in the Synod of Bishops, held at Lambeth, of Christ's Holy Catholic Church in communion with the See of Canterbury :—special, whether there are regarded evidences of the special Presence attached, and the special office of teaching the truth of God assigned, to such Synods ; or it be looked on only as a σύνοδος ἡ ἐνδημούσα, like that at Constantinople in November A.D. 448, when the Hæresiarch was formally accused of a denial of the truth of the distinction of the two natures of Jesus Christ ;—unprecedented, as the annals of our whole Communion furnish no such instance of the 'Demonstrative Unity' of its Chief Pastors. May this apostolic return by our Right Reverend Fathers in God to the earliest and normal rule and law of the Church, by which the primary signification of Christ's own words is manifestly attested and realized, exercise over the future of our one-third division of Christendom such a beneficial influence as will encourage every member of that Division gladly to recognise his position in it and to realize his 'vocation and ministry'—his calling from on high (ἡ ἄνω κλῆσις) and his office and function in the 'one Body'—as it regards that primary signification, and such as may bear comparison with that of the great Fathers of Nice over the whole history of Christendom, in the actual past and present, as well as in its probable future.

The received histories of the Catholic Church from the Day of Pentecost, after the Apostolic Synod at Jerusalem in A.D. 51, held to determine points of Ritual and to enact Canons, and another under the presidency of the Bishop of that city, held to receive a persecuted Apostle and his company, present us

with at least six recognised Œcumenical Councils or Synods—besides smaller ones—which, viewed at a mere glance, may be perhaps epitomized thus :—

		A.D.	
(1)	At NICE—318 Bishops present—it attested to 'the Deposit' and defined 'the Faith once, and once for all, delivered'—Arianism condemned—Synodical Epistle —20 Canons	325	Convoked by *Constantine the Great.*
(2)	At CONSTANTINOPLE—150 Bishops—it re-affirmed the Faith and completed the Nicene Definition—condemned the Macedonian Heresy—before it Arianism fell—7 Canons	381	Convoked by *Theodosius the Great.*
(3)	At EPHESUS—200 Bishops present—the great exposition of the Faith by S. Cyril—the Nestorian Heresy condemned—8 Canons	431	Convoked by *Theodosius the Younger.*
	At Ephesus—130 *Bishops present—Dioscorus President* .	449	*Convoked by* Theodosius *the Younger.*
(4)	AT CHALCEDON—630 Bishops—the Creed (without filioque) now set forth as perfection, τὸ τέλειον—Eutychian Heresy anathematized—Leo's Tome, rejected at Ephesus, is accepted, and Dioscorus deposed and sentenced—30 Canons	451	Convoked by *Marcian*, great lover of the Faith.
(5)	At CONSTANTINOPLE—165 Bishops—ditto—the three Chapters ; miserable results, but this Synod has always been received and respected by the Church as condemning error	556	Convoked by *Justinian* against the Church's wish and desire.
(6)	At CONSTANTINOPLE—170 Bishops—ditto—Agatho's Synodical letters—Definition of their being two natural Wills or Operations of Christ in One Person —Monothelite Error, Honorius, &c., anathematized..	681	Convoked by *Constantine IV.*
	The Quinisext Council is supplementary to the fifth and sixth, because they enacted no canons of discipline —and this made 102, confirming the doctrine of the six General Councils, 'the 85 Canons of the Apostles,' &c.—The Code of the Universal Church complete ...	692	Convoked by *Justinian II.*

At these Councils, all summoned by Imperial authority, the Holy Gospels were exalted on a Throne put in a prominent position, definitions and the transactions were regularly recorded in the Acts, and Canons enacted. The Actio was the session. A Patriarch had several Notaries attendant on him, and a Bishop always one or more. The primicerius was the Bishop's registrar. Bishops alone attested to the faith, alone determined, defined, or settled points of doctrine, declaring together by virtue of their office, 'Thus believes the Catholic Church,' and separately endorsing with 'definiens subscripsi,' whilst any other wrote 'consentiens subscripsi.' The Notaries had

to write down or copy the Acts for the Bishops, who took to their provinces the definitions of the Faith and the Canons enacted. There were also apocrisiaries, or a sort of proctors, syncelli, and promoters, and committees formed for special business, defenders and defendants, letters of citation, information demanded and declared before the Holy Gospels present so conspicuously, libels, or bills of indictment preferred against the accused, memorials, petitions, gravamina, &c., besides 'acclamations,' which formed a characteristic feature of the working of the ancient Synods, very similar, for instance, to the following :—' Such is the Faith of the Fathers. Such is the Faith of the Apostles. Peter hath spoken by Leo. So the Apostles taught. Leo hath taught piously and truly. Cyril taught so. Eternal be the memory of Cyril.' These instances of freedom include a remarkable illustration in our document.

Of these six Œcumenical Synods, the first, in the highest sense and in another, the greatest and most important, undoubtedly was that at Nicæa. Besides enacting twenty Canons, and settling for ever the questions as to the time for the Church to keep Easter and the re-admission of certain schismatics into her communion, the Fathers of the first Synod said on behalf of God's truth, and said for all Christians for all time, 'Thus believes the Catholic Church.' That General Council is the foundation on which all the others were built and grounded. The second knit itself on to it. The third affirmed 'the faith of the ᴄᴄᴄxvɪɪɪ. and of the ᴄʟ.' 'Those holy and venerable Fathers,' says S. Leo, 'who at Nice having condemned Arius with his sacrilegious impiety, enacted laws of Ecclesiastical Canons to abide to the end of the world, live in their Constitutions among us and throughout the world.' 'All the Fathers reverenced the Nicene Council, as an oracle given from heaven.' That Council also regulated the holding of Synods of Bishops. Many such Synods had taken place frequently before; and Bishop Beveridge proves, at great pains, that many were held in the second and third centuries. They were the normal rule of the Church ; and 'the *half-yearly* Synod of Bishops was then, by virtue of an authority acknowledged as supreme, appointed for the whole Church.'

During the period intervening between the first and second Œcumenical Synods, when Arianism under various phases and forms vigorously and constantly assaulted, with a view to destroy, the Faith in God the Son, but finally fell before the Faith's victory at the latter Council, we have afforded to us notices of no less than eighty Synods ; and although they were mostly unsatisfactory, being attempts to undo the work of God the Holy Ghost in the Church —waves dashing against the rocks of the true Faith, which 'foamed out their own shame,' as a Regius Professor so beautifully puts it (for I am here using his thoughts),—yet they testify to the practice of Synods of Bishops, to the

regular custom that then obtained. All the then misbelievers seem to have been such misbelievers through failing to perceive, as some do now (for Arianism under another appellative is still moribund), that 'there is no middle point between the entire Oneness of the Nature of God the Son with the Father and His being a mere creature,' since what is not God of necessity is a creature of God.

Taken together, the first four general Synods rank above all others in importance and value to the Catholic Church. They chiefly concerned themselves about 'the whole state of our Lord Jesus Christ;' to make which 'complete,' Hooker (Book V.) says, 'There are but four things that concur: His Deity, His manhood, the conjunction of both, and the distinction of the one from the other being joined in one. Four principal heresies there are which have in those things withstood the truth: Arians by bending themselves against the Deity of Christ, Apollinarians by maiming and misinterpreting that which belongeth to His human nature, Nestorians by rending Christ asunder and dividing Him into two persons, the followers of Eutyches by confounding in His person those natures which they should distinguish. Against these there have been four most famous ancient General Councils: the Council of Nice to define against Arians, against Apollinarians the Council of Constantinople, the Council of Ephesus against Nestorians, against Eutychians the Chalcedon Council. In four words, ἀληθῶς, τελέως, ἀδιαιρέτως, ἀσυγχύτως, truly, perfectly, indivisibly, distinctly; the first applied to His being God, and the second to His being Man, the third to His being of both One, and the fourth to His still continuing in that one Both: we may fully by way of abridgment comprise whatsoever antiquity hath at large handled, either in declaration of Christian belief, or in refutation of the aforesaid heresies. Within the compass of which four heads, I may truly affirm, that all heresies which touch but the person of Jesus Christ, whether they have arisen in these latter days, or in any age heretofore, may be with great facility brought to confine themselves.'

Now if there be one period in the whole of the history of the Church militant here on earth, which does or will demand of the readers of that history thoughts and reflections such as those so pithily and nervously indited in the Oxford translation of M. L'Abbé Fleury, it is that which comprises the period of heresy and the councils so succinctly reviewed and concisely summarized by Hooker. Our allusion is to the following :—'Most men who have considered the course which Church-history takes, have in some stage of their progress felt pain, if not misgiving, at the rapidity with which one heresy seems to follow upon another. To minds in this state we may suggest, first, that as wars occupy a wide space on the page of civil history, though often affording scarcely

any criterion of the aggregated happiness of a nation, so ecclesiastical history is often compelled to dwell on the life of a single heretic, while thousands and tens of thousands are passing to their heavenly inheritance unnoticed and unknown. *Secondly*, that from the disproportionate time spent in examining heresies we are apt to think too slightly of the periods of rest, those "intervals of sunshine between storm and storm" in which it "is God's will to gather in His elect little by little." *Lastly*, that heresy is overruled to several of the best ends—to promote humility—to try our faith (1 Cor. ii. 19)—to rouse the careless to an attentive study, and the religious to a more earnest realization of the Christian verities, and to subserve the evolution of those verities in a dogmatic form.'

And if there be one page in ecclesiastical history which more than another deserves and claims attention to the strikingly beautiful and thoughtful remark tersely embodying the sentiments expressed above, and placed by Dr. Burton in the forefront of his historical work, it is that which recounts the doings, especially when viewed by the additional light furnished by this ancient Syriac document, of that Patriarch of the ancient and once glorious Church of Alexandria, who marred the splendour of the Throne of SS. Athanasius and Cyril, reduced one of the grandest institutions of Christ designed for the benefit of His Church to 'the Latrocinium of Ephesus,' and so brought a withering curse upon the whole of 'the Evangelical See' of St. Mark, it may be, for ever.

It is hoped that, in this individual effort to do some honour to, and to commemorate, the Synod of Bishops of Christ's Holy Catholic Church, holden at Lambeth in September 1867, may be considered, as included, a humble desire as well to promote the study of the oldest Church language and literature generally, as to draw their attention to, if not actually to bring to bear on those many fellow Churchmen of our common 'Civitas Dei' in India, the Colonies, and other parts of the world, the rich literary Church treasures, and the accompanying advantages within easy reach, which we of the home Church possess in such great but not selfish abundance; and last, but not least, to add a little link in that chain of fraternal love that is uniting together in closer brotherhood the members of the 'One Body' living in the East and in the West, in the New World and in the Old.

S. G. F. PERRY.

TOTTINGTON PARSONAGE,
IN THE DIOCESE OF MANCHESTER
AND PROVINCE OF YORK,
September, 1867.

THE SECOND SYNOD

WHICH ASSEMBLED AT EPHESUS IN THE MONTH OF AUGUST, A.D. 449,

UNDER THE PRESIDENCY OF

DIOSCORUS

THE PATRIARCH OF THE CHURCH OF ALEXANDRIA.

d

TRANSLATION.

Imperatores Cæsares, Theodosius et Valentinianus, Victores ac Trium-
phatores, Maximi, semper Venerabiles, Augusti, Dioscoro :

Cunctis constitit manifestum quia nostræ reipublicæ status et omnia
humana, divina pietate moderantur, atque firmantur. Deo enim propitio con-
stituto, prospere et secundum vota nostra gubernari res et proficere solent. Im-
perium ergo divino motu sortiti, subditis pro pietate et mansuetudine similiter
necessario plurimam solicitudinem impertimur, quatenus et vera religio et nostra
respublica cultu Dei purissimo et pietate firmata præfulgeat. Quoniam igitur
in presenti subita emergente dubitatione, ad catholicæ et apostolicæ doctrinæ,
ac nostræ fidei custodiam, quæ, ut fit, diversis sententiis impugnata, conturbat
et confundit hominum sensus et animas ; intolerabile duximus, hujusmodi
delictum contemnere, ne per talem negligentiam ipsi Deo inferre contumelias
videremur. Ideoque sanximus, in unum sanctissimos et Deo placitos convenire
viros, quibus pro pietate catholica, atque vera fide plurimus fortasse sermo est,
ut universa quidem talis vana dubitatio, subtili proposita inquisitione solvatur,
vera autem et Deo amica fides catholica firmetur. Igitur et tua sanctitas,
sumptis secum decem reverendissimis metropolitanis episcopis, qui sub tua
degunt diœcesi, et aliis similiter decem sanctis episcopis sermone et vita ornatis,
qui in doctrina et scientia rectæ, et immaculatæ fidei apud cunctos eminent,
proximis Kalendis Augusti Ephesum Metropolin Asiæ convenire absque ulla
dilatione festinet, nullo scilicet alio præter prædictos viros sanctam synodum
molestante : quatenus universis sanctissimis et beatissimis episcopis, quos convenire per sacras nostras epistolas sanximus, ad prædictam concurrentibus
civitatem, et subtilissime investigantibus, et quærentibus, omnis de medio error
contrarius auferatur, catholica autem doctrina et orthodoxæ fidei salvatoris
nostri Christi amicissima solidetur, et consuete effulgeat : quod universi in
posterum inconcussum, Deo propitio, et intemeratum custodiant. Si quis vero

tam necessariam et Deo amicam synodum prætermiserit, et non omni virtute
secundum prædictum tempus ad præfinitum locum pervenerit, nullam excusa-
tionem neque apud Deum neque apud nostram inveniet pietatem. Sacerdotalem
enim conventum non nisi quis mala propria conscientia sauciatur evitat.
Theodoretum sane episcopum Cyri civitatis, quem pridem jussimus suæ soli
vacare ecclesiæ, sancimus non prius sanctam synodum convenire, nisi universo
sancto placuerit convenienti concilio et ipsum concurrere, et pariter interesse.
Si vero aliqua discordia de eo emerserit absque illo sanctam synodum convenire,
et quæ jussa sunt ordinare præcipimus.

> Datum tertio Kalendas Aprilis, Constantinopoli, Zenone et Postumiano
> viris clarissimis consulibus. [On the 30th of March, the third before
> (προτρεῖς) the Calends of April.]

DOCUMENTS (Depositions, &c.) against Ibas, Bishop of the City of Edessa.

[IMPERATORIS EPISTOLA AD DIOSCORUM ALEXANDRINUM.]

The Autocrat Cæsars, THEODOSIUS and VALENTINIAN, Victors and Imperators,
Illustrious, the Worshipful, the ever-August, to DIOSCORUS:

ANTEHAC quidem Theodoretum Episcopum Cyri civitatis præcepimus in
sanctam synodum minime convenire, donec de eo, quæ placuerint, synodus
sancta constituat; aversati eum, quia assumpsit proferre contraria his quæ
conscripsit de fide sanctæ memoriæ Cyrillus Alexandrinæ quondam civitatis
Episcopus. Quoniam vero suspicamur, aliquos sectatores Nestorii assumere
studium et conferre, ut omnimodo intersit sancto concilio: hac de causa neces-
sarium duximus his sacris literis uti ad tuam reverentiam, per quas manifestum
facimus tuæ beatitudini, et universæ sanctæ synodo, quod nos regulas sanctorum
patrum sequentes, non solum propter Theodoretum, sed etiam alios omnes qui
ad congregatam sanctam synodum pertinent, auctoritatem et primatum tuæ
præbemus beatitudini; scientes diligentius, quod et reverendissimus Archiepiscopus Hierosolymorum Juvenalis, et beatissimus Archiepiscopus Thalassius,
et omnis talis fervens amator et æmulator orthodoxæ fidei, consentanei erunt
tuæ sanctitati, radianti per Dei gratiam honestate vitæ et catholica fide.

Eos namque qui aliquid per additamentum aliquod, aut imminutionem
conati sunt dicere, præter quæ sunt exposita de fide catholica a sanctis patribus
qui in Nicæa, et postmodum qui in Epheso congregati sunt, nullam omnino fidu-

ciam in sancta synodo habere patimur : sed et sub vestro judicio esse volumus, quia hac de re et nunc sanctam synodum disposuimus convenire.

> This Ordinance was granted VIII Idus Augusti VI mensis die at Constantinople.

The Autocrat Cæsars, THEODOSIUS and VALENTINIAN, Victors and Illustrious in Victory, the Worshipful, the ever-August, to the HOLY SYNOD assembled at Ephesus the Metropolis :

MANY Reports (Memorials) from people at Edessa, a city in the Province of Osrhoene, with the Acts (Depositions) made there, have been sent hither, in which documents, many Reverend Clergy and God-loving Abbots and Dignitaries, and, so to speak, all the people of the city witness against Ibas, Bishop of the city of Edessa, to much impiety and blasphemy. Since then it is fitting that such profanity should be corrected by your Holiness (for, that the evidence of all these persons—Clerics and Monks and Dignitaries and Citizens—should deceive, your Holiness will assuredly not admit on reading these matters and the attestation of them), you will free the city from such blasphemy, and appoint in it a man honoured for his integrity of life, and renowned in the True Faith, as far as you can (whosoever is in his hand, in whose power the city is). And if there be any other like him in these parts who is against the Catholic Faith, let him be silenced : for, if those who preside over Metropolitan cities are orthodox, the rest will of necessity follow their teaching.

In consequence of this circumstance, therefore, we enjoined before, that the Assessors be the God-fearing Photius, Bishop of the Holy Church of Tyre, the Metropolis ; and Eustathius, Bishop of Berytus ; and Uranius, Bishop of the city of Himeria, whom also we now command to go to your Holy Synod in order to convey in person all these instructions to your Holiness.

> This Ordinance was granted the Vth of the Calends of July (Quinto Kalendas, τῇ προτέντε καλανδῶν ʼΙουλίων), which is the 27th (of June), at Constantinople.

TEMPORE—in the Consulship—Zenonis et Postumiani venerabilium consulum (sub sexto Idus Augusti), quæ secundum Ægyptios, Mesori quintadecima, (vigesima nona) indictione tertia, synodus congregata est in Epheso

e

Metropoli (in compliance with the commands of the Christ-loving Sovereigns. In the Church called Mary there sat the Venerable and God-loving Bishops, Dioscorus of Alexandria, Juvenal of Jerusalem), et Stephano Ephesi, et Thelassio Cæsareæ Cappadociæ primæ, et Eusebio Ancyræ Galatiæ primæ, [et Joanne Sebastiæ Armeniæ primæ,] et Cyro Aphrodisiadis Cariæ, et Erasistrato Corinthi Helladis, [et Quintello Heracleæ, agente etiam vices reverendissimi Episcopi Anastasii Thessalonicensis,] et Meletio Larissæ [Syriæ], agente etiam vices reverendissimi Episcopi Domni Apameæ [Cyriaco Episcopo Trocmadorum, agente vices reverendissimi Episcopi Theoctisti Pissinuntis Galatiæ secundæ], et Diogene Cyzici, ... et Basilio Seleuciæ Isauriæ, et Joanne Rhodi, [et Theodoro Tarsi, et Romano Myrorum Lyciæ,] et Photio Tyri, et Theodoro Damasci, [et Juliano Tabiæ,] et Florentio Lydiæ, et Mariniano Synnadorum, [Musonio Nyssæ,] et Constantino Bostræ, et Joanne Nicopolis Armeniæ primæ, et Acacio Ariarathiæ Armeniæ secundæ, agente vices Constantii reverendissimi Episcopi Melitenæ, et Stephano Hierapolis, et Attico Nicopolis veteris Epiri, et Eustathio Beryti, et Nunechio . . . Trimitariæ, et Olympio Constantiæ Cypri, et Candidiano Antiochiæ Pisidiæ, et Stephano Anazarbi, et Gerontio Seleuciæ Syriæ, et Rufino Samosatæ, et Indimo Hierapolis, et Timothæo Balaneæ, et Theodosiæ Canothæ, [et Eutychio Adrianopolis, veteris Epiri,] et Claudio Anthiaxi veteris Epiri, et Simeone Amidæ Mesopotamiæ, [et Eia Adrianopolis Asiæ,] et Seleuco Amasiæ, et Petro Gangræ, et Luca Dyrrhachii, et Antonio Lychnidi, et Marca Ennæ, et Vigilantio Larissæ [Macedoniæ], et Basilio Trajanopolis Rhodopæ provinciæ, et Docimasio Maroneæ Rhodopæ [provinciæ Thraciæ], et Constantino Demetriadis [Thessaliæ], et Alexandro Sebastæ Tarsi, et Sozonte Philipporum, et Eusebio Toperi Macedoniæ primæ, et Maximiano Deriensi Macedoniæ primæ, et [Hermogene Cassandriæ Macedoniæ primæ], et Luca Berrhææ Macedoniæ primæ, [et Diogeniano Bemessianensi Daciæ,] et Uranio Himerorum civitatis Provinciæ Osdroenæ, et Joanne Messenæ [civitatis Achajæ, et Theodoro Claudiopolis Isauriæ], et Athanasio Opuntinæ [civitatis] Achajæ, et Leontio Ascalonæ, et Photio Liddæ, et Anastasio Areopolis, . . . et Theodosio Amathentis civitatis, . . . et Paulo Majumensis civitatis, et Zozimo Minoidis civitatis, et Epiphanio Pergæ, et Barachia Oruxæ civitatis Palestinæ, et Heraclio Azoti, et Joanne Tiberiadis civitatis, et Musonio Zoaræ, et Dionysio Sycamazonis civitatis, et Cajumæ Phaneesis civitatis, [et Etericho Smyrnæ,] et Constantino Sebastæ, et Zebenno Pellensis civitatis, et Alypio Bostrorum civitatis, et Polychronio Antipatris civitatis, et Pancratio Libyadis civitatis, et Auxolao Sarracenorum fœderatorum, et Domnino Platearum civitatis Helladis, et Theodosio Mastaurorum civitatis, et Cyriaco Egaræ civitatis, [et Flaviano Adramytinæ civitatis,] et Cyriaco Lebedi

civitatis, et Leontio Magnæsiæ Mæandri, et Eutropio Pergami Asiæ, et Gennadio Thiensis civitatis, et Olympio Ebaganensis civitatis, et Maximo Tralliorum, et Juliano Hypæporum, et Chrysanto Balceæ civitatis, et Polycarpo Gabalorum, et Paulo Tripolis Lydiæ, ... [Meliphthongo Juliopolis, et Onesiphoro Iconii, et Longino Chersonensi civitatis, et Eudoxio Bosphori, et Timotheo Prunopolis Pamphyliæ,] et Theopompto Cabasorum, et Calosirio Arsinoitensi civitatis, et Joanne Hephæsti, et Heraclide Heracleæ, [et Isaac Elearchiensis civitatis,] et Gemellino Erythræ civitatis, et Apollonio Taneæ, et Gennadio Hermopolis majoris, et Cyro Babulinæ civitatis, et Athanasio Busiridis civitatis, ... et Theophilo Cleopatridis, et Pasmejo Parali, et Photino Tentyrenæ civitatis, et Zozimo Sozusæ, et Theodolo Ticeliæ, et Theodoro Barcæ, et Rufo Cyrenensis civitatis, et Zenone Rhinocurorum, et Lucio Zygrensis, [et Juliano Mostenæ civitatis,] et Ausonio Sebenniti, et Isaac Tavæ, et Philocalo Zagylensis et Esaia Hermopolis minoris, et Barsuma presbytero et Archimandrita, [et Longino Presbytero agente vices Dorothei Episcopi Neocæsareæ, et Anthimo presbytero agente vices Patricii episcopi Tyanorum Cappadociæ Secundæ, et Aristone presbytero agente vices Euuomii Episcopi Nicomediæ, et Olympio presbytero agente vices Calogeri Episcopi Claudiopolis Ponticæ, et Hilaro Diacono Romano, et Dulcitio Notario Romano.]

[We now come, at this early part of the MS., upon historical matter of some interest and value. Hitherto no historians have been able to record any transactions* of this Synod of Ephesus after the Session on August 8, but from the English translation which immediately follows, it will be easily discovered that there was another Session on Saturday, August 20, the proceedings of which include a resolution for the appointment of certain Bishops and Clergy to wait on the envoys of Leo and on Domnus at their private residences: and besides this we have before us palpable evidence that the Bishops assembled in Synod on the following Monday, August 22. Moreover, Fleury, after describing the exciting scene in connection with the sentence pronounced by the President of the Synod (Dioscorus) against Flavian, Bishop of Constantinople, speaks of the defective character of the then extant Acts of the Latrocinium in not recording the sentences of deposition pronounced against other Bishops besides Flavian, such as Ibas, Bishop of Edessa, and his nephew Daniel, Bishop of Charræ. It will have been noticed the case of Ibas is the first proceeding mentioned in these Acts—for this Document really records the Acts of the Synod—and it will be noticed in a few pages further on that the charge against Daniel, Bishop of Charræ, is handled. We may further point to the confirmation these next few pages afford to the stedfastness

* Except L'Abbé, t. IV. p. 1080.

of resolution and faithfulness to their trust exhibited on the part of the Roman Legates as recorded in many other ancient Documents; for their commission was simply and solely to attend to the great question affecting the True Faith. And how the Eutychian Patriarch treated Leo's letters is recorded by Fleury. The Envoys we see here remained faithful to their great Bishop, and true to their great Trust.]

John, Presbyter of Alexandria and Prime Notary, said : 'On the first day on which your holy and great Synod assembled, those who filled the place of the Venerable and God-loving Archbishop of the Church of Rome, Leo, and the God-loving Domnus, Bishop of the Church of Antioch, were missed (remained at home) and did not come.

'Your Holiness, acting in accordance with the Canons, gave order that some of the God-fearing Bishops, with some other ecclesiastical persons attendant on them, should go to them and to him (viz. the Roman Legates and Domnus), and should remind them to come to-day and assemble with your Holiness.

'Since, then, they are now here present who were sent to remind them both, that is to say, those from Rome and the God-loving Bishop Domnus, I am recalling that circumstance to your attention.'

Juvenal, Bishop of Jerusalem, said : 'Let the Holy Bishops now report the replies they received from those persons who occupy the place of the God-loving and Holy Bishop of the Church of Rome, Leo, and from the God-fearing Bishop of the Church of Antioch, Domnus.'

The God-fearing Bishops, Olympias of Evasa and Julian of Hypæpa, and Montanus Deacon of the Holy Church of Aphrodisias, and Euphronius Deacon of Laodicæa, said : 'As we were commanded by this Holy and Œcumenical Synod, we proceeded to the place where resided those persons who had been despatched from celebrated and royal Rome, who were the God-beloved Julius, Bishop, and Hilarius, Deacon. We did not, however, meet with them. Then we had an interview with Dulcitius, the Notary, who was unwell : and we said to him—"The Holy Synod has assembled, and has been retarded in the act of adjudication ;" entreating at the same time that they would likewise come to the assembly after one day, which is Monday. And the Notary replied that the God-fearing Bishop was in the town, and as for the Reverend Deacon, he was in the Church (Martyrium) of the holy and glorious John. He promised likewise to send to them to say they ought to go. However, we did not stop here, even after that conversation.

'But again in the morning of the day, which was Sunday, we proceeded thither and had an interview with the Notary, who informed us it was quite impossible for them to assemble with the Holy Synod, even if it sent ten times, in consequence of the letters with which they were accredited from Arch-

bishop Leo of far-famed and royal Rome; for there was no other commission in those letters than the order for them to go to that assembly of the Holy Synod until the affair was settled about the God-fearing Priest and Abbot Eutyches; and so those matters of which we have had cognizance we have now reported before your Holiness.'

John Bishop of Sebastia of Armenia Prima, and Onesiphorus Bishop of Iconium, and Nonnus a Deacon of Ephesus, and Phocas a Deacon of Tyre, said: 'As your Holiness commanded on the first day, which was last Saturday, we went to the holy and God-fearing Bishop Domnus of the city of Antioch, and found him prostrate on his bed and in pain, asseverating at the same time that it was on account of illness that he was wanting (in the council). We did not however rest there, but those matters which we were enjoined we communicated to him, stating to him that it was only right he should go on the day of to-day (i. e. this day) to your Holy and Œcumenical Synod. He replied readily that he would do (so), and that he prays he may assemble with your Excellencies, if he have a little respite from the sickness that holds (has seized) him.

'Then to-day, in the morning, he sent to us; and, it being proper that we should give a complete report to your Piety, we went to the said God-fearing Bishop, and found him in a miserably groaning condition, entreating at the same time that by our hands (by our means and mediation) it might be reported to your Holiness that he was, contrary to his wish and inclination, prevented from attending you (in Synod) in consequence of the debility that had seized him, and that as to what was done by your Holiness in reference to those persons who were seduced by the impieties of Nestorius or had written or were writing (such), he (Domnus) accepted your decision, and was of the same doctrine as yourselves.'

Thalassius, Bishop of Cæsarea of Cappadocia Prima, said: 'Our being detained in this city occasions much annoyance to all the God-fearing and Holy Bishops, and to the Holy Churches; nor that only, but the Gracious and Christ-loving King also wishes that there should be a rapid despatch (of the business) of this Synod, in order that he may have exact knowledge of all that is determined. Since, then, what is proper and befitting to the Holy Synod has been done;—for, they who occupy the place of the Holy and God-loving Leo, Archbishop of Rome, have been reminded by those God-loving Bishops who were sent (for that purpose, viz.) Olympias of Evasa, and Julianus of Hypæpa, and Montanus Deacon of Aphrodisias, and Euphronius Deacon of Laodicea, also the God-loving Bishop Julius, and the Reverend Hilarius Deacon, and have declined assembling here with us,—I give it as my opinion

f

that the matter be not necessarily deferred ; but if the Holy Synod command, let these matters proceed, lest the Monks too who are here be offended at the delay.'

The Imperial Cæsars, THEODOSIUS and VALENTINIAN, Victors, Triumphators, Supreme, ever-August, to the Holy Synod of Ephesus :

MANY Memorials (or Reports) from people of the city of Edessa, in the Eparchy of Osrhoene, with the Acts (or Documents) et cetera as written above.

John, Presbyter and Prime Notary, said : ' Monks who come from the city of Edessa are standing outside, and they announce that they bring us letters from the Sovereigns : what therefore does your Holiness enjoin respecting them ?'

Eusebius, Bishop of Ancyra of Galatia Prima, said : ' Let the God-fearing Bishops, Photius and Eustathius and Uranius, say what seemed good and proper to them in the cause of Ibas, and what (decisions) they have pronounced ; and because the God-fearing Priest and Head Notary John has made mention of royal letters, let those God-fearing Monks enter the Holy Synod in order to apprise it of the documents of the Gracious Kings, that have been intrusted to them.' And when they entered, John, Presbyter and Head Notary, read :—

THE AUTOCRAT CÆSARS, THEODOSIUS AND VALENTINIAN, VICTORIOUS, WORSHIPFUL, SUPREME, TO JAMES.

(Sacræ Literæ, [Barsumæ] Reverendissimo Archimandritæ destinatæ.)

VESTRAM pietatem latere non potuit, in quali sunt certamine constituti per Orientem religiosissimi et sanctissimi Archimandritæ, pro fide laborantes catholica, et quosdam episcopos in civitatibus orientis constitutos, Nestorianæ hereseos participes aversantes, collaborante etiam orthodoxo populo eisdem religiosissimis archimandritis. Quoniam igitur et tua sanctitas pro catholica fide tantum laborem sustinuit, ut ad nostram perveniret pietatem, justum esse duximus, tuam sanctitatem puritate vitæ et catholica fide probabilem (probatam), ad Ephesinam pergere civitatem, et locum tenentem omnium religiosissimorum archimandritarum orientalium, considere sanctæ synodo quæ, ibidem disposita est convenire, et cum aliis sanctis patribus et episcopis, quæ sunt Domino placita, ordinare.

Datum pridie Idus Maii in Alexandrianis.

[*Sacræ Literæ scriptæ Reverendissimo Episcopo Alexandriæ Dioscoro.*

PERVENIT ad nostræ serenitatis auditum quia multi reverendissimi orientales Archimandritæ simul cum catholicis populis adversus quosdam Episcopos, qui Nestoriana impietate ægrotare dicuntur, in quibusdam orientalium civitatibus constituti, laborarent, et pro catholica fide contenderent. Hac ergo de causa nostræ serenitati complacuit, religiosissimum presbyterum et Archimandritam Barsumam puritate vitæ et catholica fide probatissimum, adesse Ephesinæ civitati, et tenentem locum cunctorum Orientalium Archimandritarum, considere tam tuæ sanctitati, quam universis sanctissimis patribus ibidem convenientibus; quatenus Deo placita de omnibus sententia proferatur. Dignetur proinde tua religio, pervidens quia omnis nobis est pro catholica fide solicitudo, affectuose et prædictum reverendissimum Archimandritam suscipere, et operam dare, vestræ eum sanctæ synodi participem fieri.

Datæ Idibus Maii, Theralli, Protogene viro clarissimo consule, et qui fuerit nunciatus.]

[The above letter of Theodosius to the famous, or rather infamous Barsumas, which, though not a translation, contains the substance, of the Syriac letter to James, clearly shows, with it, that the Monophysite Monks who crowded to the Synod of Ephesus did not go without authority, and indicates the encouragement which the maintainers of the Monophysite Heresy received in quarters where the True Faith of the Church was professed and ought to have been upheld. This reflection is confirmed by the rescript to Dioscorus here inserted in no inappropriate manner, although it has no exact verbatim counterpart in the Syriac Text. When that Text is reproduced in its entirety, and a translation of the whole of it printed, a body of notes contemplated and rendered almost necessary by the very nature of this undertaking, will appropriately include that rescript and other similar documents. Here it may not be amiss to observe that the Editor would most thankfully receive, and afterwards acknowledge, not only a decipherment and translation of the photographic page from any Syriac scholar, but also any helps or suggestions or improvements that may be offered for the better accomplishment of a task that has few, if any, available precedents, and is attended with some by no means common or unperplexing difficulties and intricacies.]

TRANSLATION.

TRANSLATION.

‑‑‑ ❈ ‑‑‑

ܡܘܫܚܬܐ ܕܗܪܛܝܩܘ

ܕܥܠܝܬܐ ܩܘܡܐܬ ܕܬܘܝܐܕ ܠܡܢܐ ܐܡ

❖ ܕܡܘܡܥܘ ܐܡܘܡܐܐ

‑‑‑ ❈ ‑‑‑

—→→→—⬥—←←←—

ܣܘܦܣܛܘܣ ܕܐܪܝܬ

ܕܐܬܚܙܝ ܟܬܒܘܗܝ ܒܝܘܡ ܘܡܢ ܪܚܠܐ

ܘܣܘܦܣܝܐ ܐܬܘܡܐ ܀

—→→→—⬥—←←←—

ܘܩܘܝܐ ܕܐܠܗܐ. ܡܬܚܒܒܝܢ ܐܝܟ ܗܕ
ܡܛܠ ܕܐܝܬ ܟܠܗܘܢ ܒܟܠܗ ܬܒܝܠ. ܘܒܗ ܗܘ ܚܝܠܗܐ
ܐܠܗܐ ܕܗܘܘ ܐܝܟܢܐ ܡܫܘ ܗܘܐ.
ܐܦ ܡܢ ܗܘܐ ܡܛܠ ܒܪ ܡܢ ܟ ܥܠܬ ܐܝܟ
ܚܝܘܬܐ ܕܗܘܡ: ܡܢܘܬܐ ܐܘܠܝܐ ܐܘܠܝܢܐ

ܪܘܬܐܘ ܐܪܒܘ ܐܪܐܠ ܐܡܒܝ
ܐܠܒܝܡܒ ܐܢܐ ܝܢ ܐܝܪܩܗܡ
ܕܢܐܬܒܘܬܐ ܘܕܚܝܫܘܬܐ. ܠܚܠܡ ܐܡܐܪ ܀

*   *   *   *   *   *

*   *   *   *   *   *

4

o   o   o   o   o   .

     o o o o o o o

· ooooooo ·:· oooooo ·:· oooooo ·

5

10

15

20

25

      *   *   *

      *   *   *

      *   *   *

The last page of the MS. photographed awaiting and challenging decipherment and translation.

www.ingramcontent.com/pod-product-compliance
Lightning Source LLC
Chambersburg PA
CBHW021640270326
41931CB00008B/1104